golden eagle.

Shire Publications Ltd

D0486946

CONTENTS

Set in 9 point Times roman and printed in Great Britain by C. I. Thomas & Sons (Haverfordwest) Ltd, Press Buildings, Old Hakin Road, Merlins Bridge, Haverfordwest, Dyfed SA61 1XE.

ACKNOWLEDGEMENTS

I would like to thank Andrew Morant, Aero Photos, 58 Luton High Street, Chatham, Kent, for the photographs, which were specially taken for the text. I would also like to thank my mother for typing the typescript, and Robert Boucher and my husband, Steve, for their help and advice.

A 'cadge' of falcons. This device is used for carrying several hooded birds together.

A BRIEF HISTORY

Reputed to be the oldest sport in the world, falconry probably originated in China around 2000 BC. Originally it was undoubtedly devised as a method of obtaining game for the table, rather than as a sporting pastime, but the pleasures of keeping and training a hawk must have prompted the gradual westward spread of the art. About AD 860, falconry reached Britain, where, throughout its history until recent times, it has been the sport of royalty. The first English monarch to become a practising falconer was Ethelbert II. In Anglo-Saxon times there were few restrictions on hunting; virtually anybody could take a hawk from the wild and fly it wherever he chose, as the majority of the countryside was common land. However, when the Normans arrived, land came under private ownership, thereby restricting the sport to the upper classes. The sons of the gentry were taught falconry for the same reasons that they learned archery and swordsmanship — it was a noble art, and without its mastery a proper education was considered incomplete. The office of Royal Falconer was established. This post was highly respected and very well paid.

In 1486 *The Boke of St Albans* was produced. In this work a table was set out indicating that ownership of the various species of hawk was restricted to persons of certain social ranks, as follows:

An emperor—the eagle, the vulture and the 'melowne'.

A king—the gyrfalcon, or tiercel gyr.

A prince—the falcon gentill or tiercel gentill.

A duke—the falcon of the rock.

An earl—the falcon peregrine.

A baron—the bastarde.

A knight—the saker and the sacret.

A squire—the lanner and the lanneret.

A lady—the merlin.

3

A youngman—the hobby.
A yeoman—the goshawk.
A priest—the sparrowhawk.
A holywater clerk—the musket.
A knave—the kestrel.

Some of these species are not instantly recognisable and need explanation. 'Melowne' might be a term used to cover many species, implying that an emperor could also choose to fly any of the other species on the list, or, deriving from the Latin, it could mean a kite, but this seems unlikely as the kite is not a proper falconry species. The 'falcon gentill' is a name used for the peregrine, as is 'falcon of the rock', and it is possible that these two and the one referred to as 'the falcon peregrine' are subspecies of the peregrine, named differently to distinguish them.'Tiercel' means a male peregrine, taken from the French word *tierce* meaning a third, because the tiercel is one third smaller than the female falcon. The 'bastarde' has never been satisfactorarily explained: it could mean a cross-bred falcon, but this would have been unlikely in those days, or it could mean a buzzard or possibly a species hitherto unrecognised in the text. The musket is a male sparrowhawk, after which the gun was named.

We do not know how rigidly this code was adhered to, but it is certainly an indication of the value attached to birds of prey in those days. Every British king from Ethelbert II to George III practised falconry, with varying degrees of enthusiasm. Richard II created the Royal Mews for housing his falcons at Charing Cross. Later it was turned into stables by Henry VIII. When Mary Queen of Scots was imprisoned at Tutbury Castle, she was permitted by Sir Ralph Sadler to go lark hawking with her merlins — a pleasure which she was soon denied by Elizabeth I.

Interest in falconry dwindled somewhat in Britain during the eighteenth century, but by the end of the century Colonel Thornton and Lord Orford attempted to rekindle interest, introducing methods employed by the Dutch school of falconry, for by the start of the nineteenth century Holland had become the focal point for the sport in Europe.This was initiated by the Mollen family who operated from Valkenswaard. Here they set up a clearing house for the sale of their fine hand-made falconry equipment or 'furniture' and also for the sale of hawks, which they trapped, trained and sold all over Europe.

Various clubs were formed, including the Loo Hawking Club, founded in 1838, the British Old Hawking Club, which was formed in 1853 when the Loo Club was dissolved, and in 1927 the British Falconers' Club, which is still active today. Inevitably the standard of hawking is not as high now as it was in the heyday of the sport, when birds could be trapped from the wild throughout Europe and the sport pursued under lavish circumstances. However, falconry today still employs the same species, very similar equipment and training methods which have remained unchanged since the earliest days of the sport.

Saker with English Pointer. Pointers are trained to work with falcons to mark game, then spaniels are often used to flush the game when the falcon is correctly positioned above the quarry.

Car loaded for a day's hawking. A falconer's birds must become accustomed to travelling in cars in order to reach hunting grounds.

FALCONRY TODAY

The definition of falconry is the taking of wild quarry in its natural state with trained hawks and falcons. To understand how this is achieved one must understand the relationship established between a falconer and his hawk.

When a new hawk first arrives with a falconer, it is generally completely wild. The falconer's initial task is to build up the bird's trust in him with gentleness and patience, and persuade it to accept his gloved fist as a safe perch. This early stage in a hawk's training is called *manning*. Once the bird will stand on the fist indoors, a falconer must carry his hawk outdoors and start to introduce it to everything which it might encounter during its time in his care. To begin with, the hawk will *bate* and shy away from him furiously, but with the aid of two leather thongs or *jesses* fastened around the

ankles of his charge the falconer can hold his bird and gently replace it on the fist with his ungloved hand. Soon it will cease to bate for no apparent reason, attempting to leave the fist only when something specific upsets it, such as a car or a dog. In the old days a falconer would *wake* his hawk, sitting up with it day and night — sometimes for several nights — until the hawk indicated its trust in him by sleeping on his fist. Nowadays this is seldom done, as falconers have found by trial and error that hawks can be manned just as effectively with the aid of daily sessions of carriage only and can be put on a perch in the *mews* or hawk-house at night. When the hawk no longer bates away at the falconer's approach but steps calmly on to his fist to ride the glove contentedly, the falconer can progress to the next stage of training — persuading the hawk

5

to fly to him.

This next part of the training depends upon food. A hawk will not fly for a falconer to please him, or even to enjoy the exercise it affords: it can be trained only with food. Food is the principal reason for a bird flying in its wild state; fat and contented, a bird of prey will sit and wait until it is hungry again. When in captivity, therefore, it is necessary for a falconer to reduce his bird's weight to as near as possible the weight at which it would hunt in its natural state. If a hawk is too heavy it will not respond or have any inclination to fly. However, if its weight is reduced too low, then, like an athlete, a bird will not have the energy to perform well. Thus it is the falconer's task to weigh his bird daily, record that weight and make notes on the amount of

RIGHT: *Saker falcon 'ringing up' to gain the necessary height to stoop at quarry.*

BELOW: *Immature peregrine enjoying a bath. A hawk should be offered a bath every morning, leaving the bird time to dry off before being flown.*

Stooping to the lure. The lure simulates a bird in flight and the falcon is stooped repeatedly at it during daily exercise sessions, until she is fit enough for hunting.

food given and also on the performance so that he can gauge the weight at which his hawk performs best. This is called its *flying weight* and is the critical factor on which all other details of training depend. Once a hawk's weight is reduced slightly, and its appetite sharpened, the falconer can begin to encourage his bird first to feed from the fist and then to jump a short distance to his fist for food. This distance is then gradually increased, with the bird on a length of line called a *creance* to prevent it from flying off during these delicate early manoeuvres. Each flight is rewarded with a piece of meat. It is essential for a hawk to be exercised every day if it is to be trained successfully and the eventual goal of hunting achieved. When a hawk will come instantly to the falconer over a distance of 100 yards, the creance is removed and the hawk is flown free.

The training for hawks and falcons is somewhat different. Hawks take mainly ground quarry such as rabbits. They have rounded wings and relatively long tails which help them manoeuvre. They can chase their prey in fairly enclosed or wooded countryside, and their style of hunting is very direct — straight from a tree or from the falconer's fist at the quarry. Because of their rounded wings, as a group they are called *shortwings*. Falcons, however, have pointed ends to their wings and short tails and they are highly streamlined. This is because they kill other birds in mid air. They hunt by climbing to a great height and stooping down on their quarry, striking it with their feet. They are termed *longwings*.

When used for falconry, all birds of prey must be trained to take a suitable type of quarry with the use of a lure which resembles the intended prey. With hawks, therefore, this usually takes the form of a stuffed rabbit skin which is towed along the ground with a visible piece of meat tied to it to persuade the hawk to catch it, whereas falcons must be flown to a lure made out of wings, which the falconer swings on a length of line. He encourages the bird to chase this by making it stoop repeatedly at the lure. A hawk is introduced to the rabbit lure when obedience to the fist has been established, that is, when it is flying free to the fist over a distance of more than 100 yards. A falcon can be introduced to the *swung lure* much sooner, while it is still on a creance, as thereafter the lure will always be used in preference to the fist to recall it. Once a bird is responding to the lure and is reasonably fit through daily exercise, it can be *entered,* or introduced to quarry.

Hunting with a bird of prey is extremely difficult. There are many things to consider. Is the bird keen enough? Is it the right time of year to be hawking a particular quarry? Like shooting men, falconers are limited by the game seasons to the correct times for hunting. Weather, too, plays a vital part in falconry, for if it is too wet or too windy, the bird's chances are greatly reduced. Finally, a falconer must have a substantial area of suitable land available to him, with plenty of quarry to fly at, or else the sport, difficult at the best of times, will be disappointing.

Some people may think that in order to be a falconer one must merely keep a hawk. This is not true. To earn the title of falconer, a person must train and *hunt* a bird of prey. It does not suit the temperament of a raptor to keep it as one would keep a cat or a dog, within a domestic environment as a pet. They are not affectionate creatures which derive pleasure from human company. They exist to hunt and will tolerate man only as a working partner. Falconry is a highly demanding sport and unfortunately one which cannot be learnt from the pages of any book. The detailed knowledge necessary in keeping and maintaining a hawk in flying order has been imparted from generation to generation as a true skill. It can only be learned with the aid of practical demonstration from an experienced falconer.

The author and a ferruginous buzzard returning from an afternoon's hunting.

Aylmeri jesses with leash. Aylmeris were invented by Major Guy Aylmer as an alternative to the traditional one-piece jesses, the straps of which could not be removed when the bird was flying free.

THE EQUIPMENT

Most of the equipment used in the sport has remained virtually unchanged since the earliest days of falconry. Much of it is made out of leather, and each piece has to be crafted individually for the hawk it is designed to fit. The various items of 'furniture', as the equipment is correctly termed, are as follows:

THE JESSES
These are two straps of equal length made of leather. They are fitted comfortably around the hawk's legs in such a way that they cannot tighten. They are used to retain the hawk on the fist and are greased regularly for suppleness.

AYLMERIS
These are a modern type of jesses. They take the form of leather anklets fastened around the bird's legs with metal eyelets through which leather 'button jesses' are passed. When the bird is flown free, the button or 'mews' jesses can either be removed completely or replaced by small field jesses, which decrease the possibility of the bird getting caught up on a fence or in a tree.

THE SWIVEL
This is attached to the jesses to prevent them from becoming twisted. It is made of two metal rings joined on a swivelling stem. The jesses are attached to the larger ring.

THE LEASH
The leash is put through the smaller ring of the swivel. It is approximately 1 metre (39 inches) in length and is used to tether the hawk when it is not being exercised. Traditionally leashes were made of leather but nowadays falconers usually prefer to use braided nylon as it is stonger and does not crack as leather will when it gets wet.

BELLS
Bells are attached to trained hawks so that the falconer can hear his bird when it is out of sight. The bells are generally made of weak brass and have a good tone. They are specially made for hawks in pairs, there being a difference in pitch

of roughly a semitone between the two bells of a pair. This combination produces a vibrant tone which can be heard over a greater distance than a more melodious mixture would be. The bells are usually attached one to each leg by leather straps called *bewits*, so when the hawk moves about in a tree the bells can be heard. Some species of hawk have a habit of shaking their tails so on these species one bell is mounted at the top of the tail. Similarly, others bob their heads, so the bell is put round the neck.

TELEMETRY

One of the few modern pieces of equipment now being widely used in falconry is radio tracking equipment called 'telemetry'. It takes the form of a small, lightweight transmitter, which is attached to the leg or tail of a hawk, and from which a short aerial wire trails. With the aid of a tracking unit and antenna the falconer can trace the signal transmitted by the equipment on the hawk, over a restricted range. This is a technological advance which all falconers appreciate as it has resulted in many valuable hawks being recovered when they would otherwise have been lost.

HOODS

The hood is the temporary blindfold placed over the hawk's eyes to keep it quiet and to protect it from an environment which might otherwise upset it. It takes the form of a lightweight leather cap which is measured to fit snugly over the head, leaving a hole for the beak to protrude. At the base of the hood there is a system of interwoven leather braces, enabling the hood to be opened and closed. There are many different designs of hood from all over the world. Some are plain in design and colour, whilst others are elaborately tooled and decorated. In medieval times the colours over the eyepieces of the Dutch design of hood denoted the type of game at which the

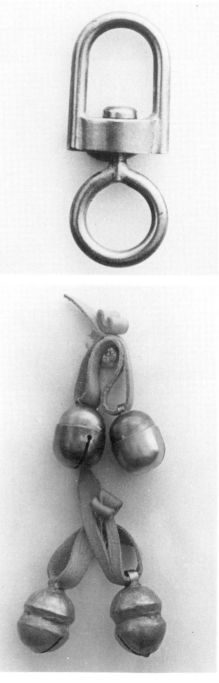

TOP RIGHT: *A swivel. This is attached between the jesses and the leash to prevent them from becoming twisted. Many different designs have been tried, but the 'D' swivel pictured here has proved to be one of the most successful.*

RIGHT: *Bells. These are attached to the hawk's legs so that the falconer can hear his bird when it is out of sight.*

ABOVE: *A Dutch hood. Called 'the hood proper', this type of hood is beautifully made with coloured side panels and a feather plume.*
ABOVE RIGHT: *A 'Bahreini' or Arabic hood. This design is used by Arabic falconers, mainly on saker falcons.*

RIGHT: *An Anglo-Indian hood. This is a simple design which can be drawn up to fit the head of virtually any species of raptor from a single measurement.*

Hooding. TOP LEFT: *The hood is shown to the bird.*
TOP RIGHT: *It is slipped gently over the head.*
ABOVE LEFT: *The braces are drawn.*
ABOVE RIGHT: *The falcon is at ease.*

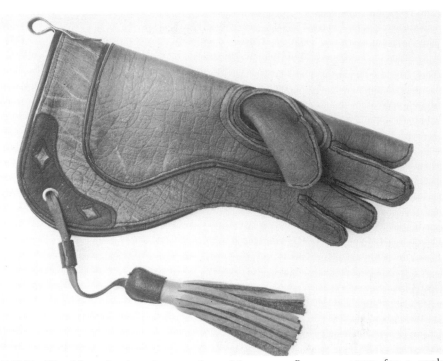

ABOVE: *The falconer's glove is generally worn on the left hand, leaving the right hand free.*
BELOW: *A hawking bag. This is used to carry meat, spare swivels, leash, lures and so on.*

falcon was flown — green for a rook hawk, rcd for a game hawk, and purple for a bird that had taken heron.

GLOVES

The talons of a bird of prey are very sharp and powerful, so a falconer must wear a leather glove to protect his hand from the grip of his hawk. The glove varies in size and thickness according to the type of bird a falconer is handling. For example, a glove for a merlin or kestrel is adequate if it reaches the wrist and it must be quite soft and thin to enable the falconer to handle the bird with sensitivity, whilst the glove for an eagle must extend to the elbow to accommodate the span of the bird's feet, and it must be thick and fairly stiff to prevent the falconer's hand becoming bruised by the eagle's powerful grip. Good gloves are made from best quality hide such as a good buckskin. They are regularly greased to protect the leather.

BAG

When out hunting, a falconer wears a

bag to carry the meat used to recall the hawk, the lure and various other accoutrements such as a whistle, spare swivel and leash, and also the game which the hawk kills. It usually has different compartments for these items. It also has a holder for field jesses. Leather has been superseded by canvas as the material for bags.

LURES

As already described, lures resemble

A rabbit lure. This is baited with meat and dragged along the ground to train a hawk to hunt rabbits.

A swung lure. This is made by drying the wings of the intended quarry species and mounting them back to back.

A bow perch. These perches are designed to be like the branches on which a hawk would perch in its natural state.

the bird's intended prey. Rabbit lures are made out of rabbit skins stretched over pieces of padded wood. A line is attached at one end so that the lure can be towed along the ground. A swung lure is made out of a pair of wings stitched back to back and swung on a length of braided nylon line.

CREANCE
The creance is a length of nylon line approximately 50 metres (54 yards) long, which is attached to the hawk's swivel during the early stages of training.

BLOCKS AND PERCHES
Various types of perches are used for birds of prey and have been designed to resemble the perching surfaces on which the birds would usually sit in the natural state. Falcons perch on cliffs and rock faces, so they are given a flat-topped *block perch* on which they can sit flat-footed, hooking their front or back talons over the sides of the block. Hawks, however, generally perch in trees, so their perches are designed like branches which they can grip around. Thus we have the *bow perch* and the *ring perch* which are made from circular lengths of wood or padded metal. All the perches have a tethering ring to which the leash is tied.

SCALES
An accurate pair of balance scales is essential to enable the falconer to weigh his hawk daily. It must be accurate to a quarter of an ounce (7 grams).

Many other small items are necessary for a falconer: a complete set of leather tools is essential. There are specialist equipment suppliers who make and market furniture specifically for falconry. This is a great help to those falconers who do not have the facilities, ability or patience to make all of their own equipment.

TOP RIGHT: *A block perch. This type of perch is used for falcons and is generally topped with cork or Astroturf to provide a surface which is suitable for the feet to perch on.*
RIGHT: *When hawks are being trained, they are weighed every day. The old-fashioned type of balance scale is more accurate for weighing birds than spring balance scales.*

A kestrel. These birds are not proper falconry birds and are unsuitable for beginners.

ABOVE LEFT: *The common buzzard is ideal as a first bird.*
ABOVE RIGHT: *Goshawks are undoubtedly the best hawks for hunting, but they are moody and difficult to maintain.*

THE BIRDS

It is impossible to mention all the birds flown for falconry throughout the world, but some of the most popular species are described here. The birds thought suitable for beginners are discussed first, and then the others, divided into their relative groups.

THE KESTREL
Falco tinnunculus
The kestrel is commonly thought of as the ideal beginner's bird. This is a misconception. They are delicate little falcons which are too small to undergo the necessary weight-loss process safely during training in inexpert hands. Beginners are therefore better advised to start with a bird that is a little more substantial. They are not proper falconry birds in a strict sense as they cannot usually be flown at quarry with much success. However, as a second bird they have much to offer a falconer who wishes to progress eventually to the larger long-

wings. This is because kestrels are flown to the lure during training in exactly the same manner as a large falcon, thus providing an ideal partner for a falconer who needs to master the art of swinging the lure.

THE COMMON BUZZARD
Buteo buteo
Buzzards are ideal hawks for a beginner. They are considerably bigger than kestrels and much more robust. They are therefore able to withstand the small mistakes which beginners will inevitably make. For example, a kestrel weighs only about 6 to 8 ounces (170-230 grams), needing to lose maybe a mere 1½ ounces (40 grams) to achieve its flying weight. A buzzard weighs approximately 2 pounds (910 grams) if male and 2½ pounds (1130 grams) if female and usually needs its weight to be reduced by about 6 ounces (170 grams) in order to perform well. Thus the margin for error is much greater

with the buzzard: a mistaken reduction overnight of an extra quarter ounce (7 grams) might well prove fatal for a kestrel but would probably be inconsequential for a buzzard. Buzzards have a relatively steady temperament. They are not particularly fast or impressive in flight, but in the hands of an able and determined beginner they can be persuaded to take a variety of quarry, including rabbit, moorhen and squirrel.

SHORTWINGS
THE SPARROWHAWK
Accipiter nisus

The name sparrowhawk is often mistakenly applied to kestrels. Kestrels are the birds seen hovering over motorways — indeed they are the only British species that can hover. Sparrowhawks are rarely seen in the wild state as they dart along hedgerows and keep well away from human activity. As falconry birds, sparrowhawks are extremely difficult to manage. Like the kestrel, they are small and delicate, but they have the additional problem of having a very nervous temperament, which usually makes them infuriatingly awkward to train and maintain over a long period. They are thus best left to experienced falconers who have a great deal of patience and the necessary sensitivity of touch. They are exceptionally good hunting birds. Given the nickname of 'hedgerow bandit', they are flown off the fist at small birds up to the size of moorhens.

THE GOSHAWK
Accipiter gentilis

The goshawk is a larger version of the sparrowhawk, having the same temperament but a slightly more robust frame. They are excellent hunting birds, although they too are suitable only for experienced falconers. Their performance in terms of speed is unmatched by any of the other shortwings. They take a wide variety of quarry including rabbit, moorhen, squirrel, duck, pheasant, partridge and hare.

THE REDTAILED BUZZARD
Buteo jamaicensis

Redtails are the American equivalent of common buzzards and are therefore used by beginners in the United States. They are not as readily obtainable in Britain and are therefore usually obtained as a second shortwing after a buzzard. They are better hunting birds than common buzzards, being both larger and faster. They can take rabbit, moorhen, squirrel, pheasant and hare.

THE FERRUGINOUS BUZZARD
Buteo regalis

These are birds of striking appearance from western North America. They are similar in terms of performance to a redtail but have more the temperament and size of a small eagle.

THE HARRIS HAWK
Parabuteo unicinctus

Harris hawks are excellent and versatile shortwings. They have a remarkably amicable temperament and an outstanding hunting ability. They would be ideal as beginners' birds, but unfortunately, being hard to obtain, they are very highly prized in Britain and are therefore beyond the reach of the average beginner. They take the same quarry as a goshawk, and although they are not quite as fast on the wing their comparatively easy-going nature more than makes up for this failing.

LONGWINGS
THE PEREGRINE FALCON
Falco peregrinus

Peregrines are probably the most highly esteemed birds in falconry circles. Known throughout the world for their beauty and speed in flight, they are much sought after and treasured by falconers. In Britain they are generally flown as either rook hawks or game hawks. A rook hawk requires a totally different style of flight and consequently form of training to a game hawk. Rook hawks are trained to stoop to the lure in the manner previously described. This builds up their muscle and stamina to enable them to be flown 'out of hood' off the fist at rooks. Game hawks, however, are never stooped to the lure as this would prevent them from reaching sufficient height to enable them to take game. Game hawking is the most difficult and demanding of

Redtailed buzzards are used as beginners' birds in America.

The ferruginous buzzard is a very large member of the buzzard family. Females reach the size of the smaller species of true eagle.

The harris hawk is an excellent hunting bird with a very amiable disposition.

all forms of the falconer's art. For grouse hawking it is necessary to have excellent open moorland of the type found in northern Scotland, in areas such as Caithness; steady working dogs such as setters and pointers are needed to mark game, and every detail such as the position and height of the falcon, the direction of the wind, and the moment of flush must be correct if a kill is to be achieved. The falcons, or female peregrines, are generally flown at grouse, whilst the smaller tiercels, or males, are normally flown at partridge during their first season.

THE LANNER FALCON
Falco biarmicus

Lanner falcons come from Africa. They are slightly smaller than peregrines and do not fly as well. However, they are popular for falconry as they fly well to the lure and can be persuaded to take various prey including rook, mallard, magpie and, in their native Africa, small game birds such as francolin.

THE LUGGER FALCON
Falco jugger

Luggers come from India and Pakistan. They are very similar to lanners in size and appearance. They fly well to the lure but are seldom flown at quarry in Britain as they are less enthusiastic about taking game than lanners. However, the lugger makes an excellent first large falcon with which an inexperienced longwing man can perfect the arts of hooding and lure-swinging, before he progresses to a longwing with greater hunting potential.

THE GYRFALCON
Falco rusticolus

Gyrfalcons are highly prized. They enjoy the reputation of being the fastest, largest and most beautiful longwings in the world. They are rarely encountered in Britain, as they are extremely valuable and hard to obtain.

THE SAKER FALCON
Falco cherrug

Sakers are large loose-feathered falcons which are generally associated with Arabic falconry. In the Middle East they are flown at 'houbara' or McQueen's bustard, and desert hare. They are well suited to hunting in the desert as they come from hot countries and are thus able to withstand and work in the climate there.

THE MERLIN
Falco columbarius

Merlins are Britain's smallest native falcon. They are quite rare now, both in the wild and as falconer's birds. Being extremely small, they, like sparrowhawks, require a delicate touch. They are flown mainly at skylarks. Skylark hawking, which is permitted only if the necessary licence is obtained, is a spectacular sport. The lark rings up, with the merlin

Lanner falcons originate from Africa, where they are used for hunting small game birds such as francolin.

The peregrine falcon is known throughout the world for its speed and power in flight.

The author with a gyrfalcon, the largest species of falcon in the world.

ABOVE LEFT: *Saker falcons are reputed to have been flown by Arab falconers at gazelle and were worked in conjunction with Saluki hunting dogs.*
ABOVE RIGHT: *In the middle ages merlins were flown by ladies because they were small and their weight could easily be borne by a lady during a day's hawking on horseback.*

competing for altitude. If the merlin gains enough height, it puts in many stoops at the lark, which is generally taken on the ground. The season is short — from the beginning of August until the end of the third week of September, after which the larks are too strong on the wing to be caught by the best of merlins.

EAGLES

Eagles are rarely used for serious hawking as they are cumbersome to carry around, slow off the mark and difficult to train.

THE GOLDEN EAGLE
Aquila chrysaetos

These magnificent birds are usually temperamental when trained for falconry. They tend to be 'one-man birds', requiring great dedication and single-mindedness from a falconer in order to cope with the problems that they present. They have great powers of fasting, making it very difficult to find their flying weight. They are hard to get fit, and they

lose condition very rapidly if they are not worked consistently. When trained they will take large ground game up to the size of a fox.

TAWNY AND STEPPE EAGLES
Aquila rapax rapax and *Aquila rapax nipalensis* or *Aquila rapax orientalis*

These are smaller relatives of the golden eagle, originating from Africa. They are of a more manageable size, but they have limited usefulness as hunting birds.

HAWK EAGLES

Hawk eagles are rather like a cross between eagles and true hawks, hence their name. They are usually very aggressive towards quarry (and often towards falconers too). They are better shaped as falconry birds than true eagles, as, sitting more upright on the fist, they are built for short sharp bursts of speed and are equipped with good feet for holding quarry such as hares and game birds.

25

The golden eagle is used in falconry to hunt rabbit, hare and occasionally foxes.

The tawny eagle is an African species, but it is more commonly flown in Britain than in Africa.

Steppe eagles are a larger sub-species of the tawny eagle.

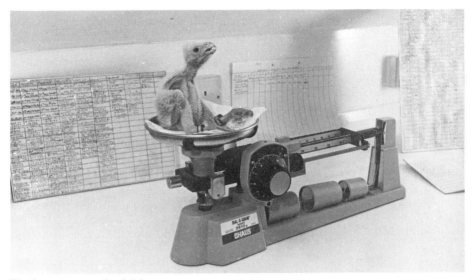

Weighing a captive-bred falcon to monitor its daily weight gain.

CONSERVATION

As with so many forms of wildlife, the conservation of birds of prey is an important issue. The loss of habitat and, in many cases, the damage to prevalent food supply is a serious problem. However, falconers have made a determined effort in recent years to combat the decline in numbers of wild populations by breeding endangered species in captivity. This work requires the devotion of time, money and effort as it is by no means easy to persuade raptors to reproduce under artificial conditions. Through the work of dedicated individuals new techniques in the fields of artificial insemination, incubation and rearing have been devised. New developments are made each year, and although falconers can never be totally self-sufficient in terms of producing all their own stocks for future hunting and breeding, because of the need for fresh blood, many birds are now being bred annually to help to satisfy the needs of falconers without reaping the wild stocks, and, in many cases, for release to the wild. These techniques have been of particular value in the Mauritian kestrel breeding programme and the Philippine eagle breeding project, and also in the Peregrine Fund

for the release of peregrines in America. It is extremely encouraging that falconers can make such a positive contribution to conservation.

Under British law all birds of prey are protected. It is necessary to obtain a licence from the Department of the Environment in order to take one from the wild or to import one. Under the Wildlife and Countryside Act of 1982 a system of registration has been introduced for all diurnal birds of prey in captivity. All legally held raptors have a government band on their leg bearing a unique number with which they are registered to their keeper. Records are kept at the Department, which must be notified of any transfer of keepership. Also every young bird bred in captivity has a government numbered closed ring placed on its leg. In this way the Department can keep a check on the birds being held in captivity, thus helping to prevent illegal taking from the wild.

There is pressure on field sports from opponents of blood sports. Fortunately this can in no way be applied to falconry. The taking of quarry by birds of prey is a natural occurrence which takes place every day in the wild. A bird trained for

ABOVE: *The weathering ground at the British School of Falconry.*

BELOW: *The incubation room at the British School of Falconry. Captive breeding of birds of prey is playing a significant role in modern falconry.*

falconry makes far fewer kills than it would do in its natural state. Moreover, once a bird is on the wing, there is no way that a falconer can assist it with any artificial or unsporting aid; the chase that follows is purely between the hawk obeying its instincts and wild prey being pursued in its natural habitat. Through the ages man has been fascinated by birds of prey and has learned of the special relationship that can be established between man and hawk. The sport of the fortunate but dedicated people who practise falconry today is as natural as it was during its eastern origins thousands of years ago.

Feeding a young lanner falcon.

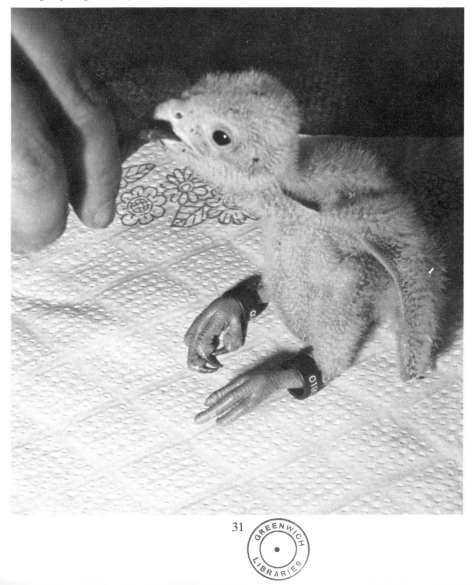

PLACES TO VISIT
The Bird of Prey Conservation and Falconry Centre, Newent, Gloucestershire GL18 1JJ. Telephone: Newent (0531) 820286.
The Hawk Conservancy, Weyhill, Andover, Hampshire SP11 8DY. Telephone: Weyhill (026 477) 2252.
The Welsh Hawking Centre, Weycock Road, Barry, South Glamorgan CF6 9AA. Telephone: Barry (0446) 734687.

FURTHER READING
Allen, Mark. *Falconry in Arabia.* Orbis, 1980.
Ford, Emma. *Birds of Prey.* Batsford, 1982.
Ford, Emma. *Falconry in Mews and Field.* Batsford, 1982.
Glasier, Philip. *Falconry and Hawking.* Batsford, 1978.
Mavrogordato, Jack. *A Hawk for the Bush.* Neville Spearman, 1960.

FALCONRY COURSES
The British School of Falconry, Stelling Minnis, Canterbury, Kent CT4 6AQ. Telephone: Stelling Minnis (022 787) 575. The school run by the author and her husband. Falconry courses available (residential and non-residential) at beginners' and advanced levels.

CLUBS AND SOCIETIES
The British Falconers' Club, c/o J. Chick (secretary), Moonrakers, Allington, Salisbury, Wiltshire SP4 0BX.
Northern England Falconry Club, c/o B. Thelwell, 2 Fourlands Drive, Lolle, Bradford, West Yorkshire BD10 9SJ.
The Welsh Hawking Club, c/o Mrs Ann Shuttleworth, 21 North Close, Blackfordby, Burton upon Trent, Staffordshire DE11 8AP.

EQUIPMENT SUPPLIERS
Robin Haigh, Abbey Bridge Farm House, Colonel's Lane, Chertsey, Surrey KT16 8RJ.
Martin Jones, The Lodge, Huntley, Gloucester GL19 3HG.
Ben Long, 59 Church Road, Long Hanborough, Oxford OX7 2JF.

TELEMETRY
Robert Boucher, Vega Electronics, Nouds Farm, Lynsted, Sittingbourne, Kent ME9 0ES.

REGISTRATION AND LICENCES
Department of the Environment, Tollgate House, Houlton Street, Bristol BS2 9DH.